THE OLD REFORMATION AND THE NEW

THE OLD REFORMATION AND THE NEW

The Cato Lecture for 1966

GORDON RUPP

FORTRESS PRESS PHILADELPHIA

First published by Epworth Press, London, 1967

Library of Congress Catalog Card Number 67-21530

5565D67 Printed in U.S.A. 1-1364

For

Eric and Lorna Osborn

'The Voice of the Lord is powerful:
The Voice of the Lord is full of majesty:
The Voice of the Lord breaketh the cedars.

. . . . . .

The Voice of the Lord cleaveth the flames of fire,
The Voice of the Lord shaketh the wilderness.'

Psalm 29

'The sheep follow him; for they know his Voice. And a stranger will they not follow, but will flee from him; for they know not the voice of strangers.'

John 10[45]

'Today we live in an age of miracles, when history seems to have been overtaken. The events of the 16th century are being looked at in the new light of the 20th.'

Dr. Una Porter (formerly Miss U. Cato)

THE Cato Lectureship is more than an academic foundation. In the generous vision of the late Fred J. Cato it was instituted for the procreation of spiritual children and for the mutual society, help and comfort that two great Churches ought to have one of the other. The Cato Lecturer is more than a visiting lecturer, for he is a status symbol. His status is that of an ambassador, and he is received with a wealth of kindness, and an honour which, if he is wise, he recognizes as having no relation at all to his own personal qualities, but to be indeed the symbol and expression of the brotherly love between the Methodist Church of Australia, and the world family of Methodism. Among so many kind and generous friends, it is invidious to mention any names, but I cannot in decency omit those of the retiring President-General, Dr Frank Hambly, of the President-General himself, the Rev. Cecil Gribble, and the most courteous and thoughtful director of the whole operation, the Secretary-General, the Rev. C. K. Daws.

In a gracious speech of welcome, on behalf of the Cato family, Dr Una Porter used words which I took to be an inspired premonition of the theme of my Lecture and I have printed her sentences in this book. Long may this happy traffic between our Churches continue. It will be in no sense one way.

This lecture includes material previously given in the Birks Lectures at McGill University, Montreal, in 1965, and in sermons preached before the Universities of Oxford and Cambridge.

GORDON RUPP

Feast of the Transfiguration of Our Lord, 1966

Contents

CHAPTER ONE

An Age of Revolution

'It was the best of times, it was the worst of times, it was the age of wisdom, it was the age of foolishness, it was the epoch of belief, it was the epoch of incredulity, it was the season of light, it was the season of darkness, it was the spring of hope, it was the winter of despair, we had everything before us, we had nothing before us, we were all going direct to heaven, we were all going direct the other way—in short, the period was so far like the present period that some of its noisiest authorities insisted on its being received, for good or for evil, in the superlative degree of comparison only.'

CHARLES DICKENS: *A Tale of Two Cities*

THAT ours is an age of revolution is the obvious platitude of our time. Wherever you look, there is swift, accelerating change. In science, a bursting storm of new learning, as we enter the atomic age with its engrossing possibilities: the space age, with its impressive technological background, its infinite prospects, and its unfolding implications, not least for our ideas about the universe and the place of man within it. In the political field, in Africa and Asia, the ferment of new nationalisms, new groupings of political and economic power. Or there are the horizontal tensions between East and West, the population explosion, the educational revolution. Impressive, glittering with promise: yet shot through and through with ominous foreboding, so that it is revolution tinged with apocalyptic: for behind it all is the Bomb: the possibility that our age might end, as man began, in the caves and amid the catacombs.

It is always well to stand back a little when looking at a

picture. If we would understand what is happening in the world around us, we must look back at least to the 17th century, to the loosening of modern Europe from what had been Christendom: to what Paul Hasard called 'the crisis of European conscience' of a century which began, as he says, by believing with Bossuet and ended by doubting with Voltaire. Here is the claim of modern man to plan his existence, free from supernatural discipline, appealing to reason rather than faith and to science rather than religion. And so ushering in that age of 'Enlightenment', of which much of what is called 'the New Reformation' is the latest reverberation.

In the 17th century, too, there is the first articulate voice of modern revolutionary man. In the Puritan Civil War, perhaps in those astonishing debates between Cromwell's soldiers, there is a new appeal to natural law, no longer as the prop of a static society based on duties but as a revolutionary idealism, based on human rights. This runs as a kind of virus through the American War of Independence, the French Revolution, and the Liberal European Revolutions of 1830 and 1848, and even among the dynamisms of Fascism and Nazism. Not the least important fact about Communism is that within it there has been an unresolved tension between a 'Rights of Man' idealism and the ideological system of Karl Marx.

What of the Church? In recent years two surveys of the last 150 years, by the American historian Latourette and the English scholar A. R. Vidler, have made a similar point. The great questions in this period have not, they say, been pressed on modern man by the Church, out of its own inner life, its dialogue with the Gospel, but they have come from the world outside, out of the pressures of history, out of the height and depth and poignancy of unprotected human experience.

When we look at Christian Churches throughout this

period, the application to them of the word 'revolutionary' seems almost grotesque. We know very well what revolutionaries look like. There are enough bad pictures in Moscow and Leningrad to show us. But no such scruffy-looking mobs stream out of Church House or the Vatican or the Château Bossey hustling defaulters through the streets to the cry 'A la lanterne!' And as we look round at our Christian selves in our local church or at an ecumenical conference, the word 'revolution' doesn't fit. As the lady in the hat shop says: 'It just isn't you, modom.' The first Christians—the first Franciscans—the first Methodists—ah, that is another story.

One of the obvious things about revolution is its pace, and therefore its toughness. Changes which might normally and naturally demand years to work out have to be rushed through in weeks, sometimes in hours. It is like a river in flood, swiftly increasing its pressure to the point of near disaster, of rough and ruthless force. When this happens, good things get lost and nice people get hurt.

Even so, our world rushes on its way, with the swift ticking of the second hand of a watch, while within the Church we seem to chime the hours. We go on our decorous 19th-century way as though we had all the time in the world to postpone decisions. We talk of Christian unity as something which will inevitably happen 'in God's good time'—which invariably means painlessly, and at the pace of the die-hards. It is all dangerously reminiscent of Marie Corelli who refused to accept Summer Time because, she said, God's time was good enough for her, and so she set the clocks in her house differently from those of the world outside.

But in a world on the move and on the march, the Church too must learn a new rhythm. Like unjust stewards we must sit down and write quickly, agree with our adversary along the road. For in the end it is not simply a question of catching up with the spirit of the age, of keeping pace with the world, but with a God who is marching on, ahead of us all.

Winston Churchill has a striking sentence about Lawrence of Arabia and the way in which, in World War I, he found his hour. 'The fury of the Great War,' he said, 'raised the pitch of life to the Lawrence standard. The multitudes were swept forward until their pace was the same as his.' Is not this a clue to the relation of history to Jesus of Nazareth? Does he not, too, take destiny by the throat? Newman has these perceptive words about the urgent rhythm of the Christian liturgy, the pace of Christian words:

> 'They hurry on, as if impatient to fulfil their mission. Quickly they go, for the whole is quick. Quickly they pass, for the Lord Jesus goes with them, as He passed along the lake in the days of His flesh, quickly calling first one and then another. Quickly they pass, because as the lightning which shineth from one part of the heaven to the other, so is the coming of the Son of Man.'

Aware of the laggard Christian pace, conscious of the quickening rhythm of the age, it is no wonder that Christian men have turned to remember the moments of crisis and creative change in the Christian past. Or that to the sounding brass of 'De Ecumenismo' should be added the tinkling cymbal of the Bishop of Woolwich in the cry of a 'New Reformation'. I am not here concerned with his tract; indeed, I have taken good care to read it only as a man who runs may read, or rather as a man may meditate over a cup of tea in Lyon's.

Rather I take my own text, from a University Sermon which I preached in 1947 about the Protestant Martyrs of the University of Cambridge, when I said something like this:

> 'Nobody living in the year 1509 could have foreseen that, before he died, there would come into existence new patterns of Christian life

worship and proclamation, new institutions of Christian piety and discipline, and these not only in the new churches of the Reformation, but in the Catholic Church, too.'

And I added:

'Now these creative works of the Reformation seem to be coming to an end as vehicles of effective evangelism and communication. If our gospel is to come home to the estranged millions of modern men, those great first works may need to be done again.'

The Book of Common Prayer, the Authorized Version of the Bible, the 39 Articles, the Westminster Confession, these are the kind of works which need to be done again. They are, of course, still living classic documents which have worn pretty well through four centuries. Nor are they just to be put away as museum pieces, of meaning only to antiquarians or aesthetes. Yet, properly understood, these very classic documents are part of the evidence why, in our day, we may need to make new liturgies, new translations, new confessions.

Let us not either, in turning to the 16th century, beg an important question—whether in fact there are other centuries, other periods of modern history more relevant, more deserving of our close attention. At least a good case can be made out (with support from Troeltsch and Butterfield) for the view that the period 1650–1750 is the real breakthrough of the modern world, more pertinent to the present, while a good deal of what is called 'the New Reformation'—not least its rather naïve self-confidence and its romanticizing of unbelief, would more appropriately be called 'the New Enlightenment'.

'The New Reformation'—it is too late to appeal against a slap-happy use of a great metaphor, but perhaps not too late to examine the meaning and relevance of that figure of speech against the historical and theological facts. For it is the second-rate historian who dashes in and out with imagined parallels and lessons from the past. But if we rush back into history with our own questions and pre-occupations we make the past a mere sounding-board for our own ideas, and substitute for the enthralling dialogue between generations a ventriloquial monologue through straw puppets of our own devising.

To put the analogy between the Old and the New Reformations under a microscope may seem unjustifiable pedantry, but those who have lightheartedly taken it to themselves can hardly complain if their bluff is called. Having appealed to history, to history they must go, and it is a little late in the day to complain, in effect: 'Ah, but we are prophets not historians.'

Indeed a historian is, as Herbert Butterfield has said, just a man sitting at a desk and, by that token, a Church historian might be called a man sitting at a prayer desk (Methodist posture!). But at any rate, he is not just a collector of antiquated rubbish, his mind a disordered Old Curiosity Shop. It is his task to be the remembrancer of mankind. And this must always be a chancy, and haphazard, affair, for he cannot know whether the important clues may not have disappeared.

There was a cartoon in *Punch* of a polar expedition, and one of the party cries out: 'We're nearly there! I can see the B.B.C. Television cameras waiting to greet us!' But contrast the poignancy of the scrap of paper in the British Museum, Captain Scott's last message to the world: 'For God's sake look after our people'—which so easily might have been lost for ever.

Historians, like those of other crafts and disciplines, may take themselves too seriously. When they get together you hear them talking of 'balanced judgements' and 'historical perspective', and then it is salutary to remind them that the philosophers and the mathematicians and the scientists are wont to make much the same claims for their own disciplines. But there is something in it.

'Balanced judgement' at the lower end of the scale may stand for the dilettantism of the academic mind, for the evasion of prophetic action, for the man who flies to his packet of historical labels whenever there is danger of meeting a new idea, rather like a very young medical student who might flee to his textbook and be more jubilant to have made his diagnosis and found the name of the disease than if he had made a cure. But rightly to discriminate between the present and the past, to press home an historical analogy does indeed demand a knowledge, a skill and a delicacy comparable with that of a surgeon operating on a brain. This is clear when we turn to the great historians. They really do call old worlds into being to redress the balance of the new. And even a working historian may have his use at a time like the present, of publicity explosions, and of theological band-waggons. He at least ought not to be shocked or surprised, or swept off his feet, and should be among the last to panic. And then, there is something in this business of historical perspective. The historian is made a freeman of the centuries, disengaged from the persistent fallacy of automatic progress, aware that Plato and Shakespeare and Beethoven and Wordsworth had perceptions of truth and beauty beyond most of us, and therefore for him there is a genuine continuing dialogue between the generations. There is much in the life of our own day which is peculiar to it—this was true of ancient Athens and medieval London. There are questions we must raise for ourselves and answer by ourselves, to which the voices of other generations are, to coin a phrase, irrelevant and immaterial. But there are other questions, and these the most profound, which touch all human experience, and to answer which involve us in a continuing dialogue which we did not begin and which will go on after us, and then it may be that Augustine or Pascal or Dostoievski or Péguy may disconcertingly and freshly intervene. Indeed if there is a Christian message which has meaning for all men at all times, then an hour of crisis like the 16th century, a time when men were plunged into an emergency world of desperate improvisation, may have quite urgent relevance for us, might, in the old phrase, speak to our condition. It is worth taking a long look at that Old Reformation.

PART I

The Old Reformation

'Take me, for example. I opposed indulgences and all papists, but never by force. I simply taught, preached, wrote God's Word; otherwise I did nothing. And then while I slept or drank Wittenberg beer with my Philip and my Amsdorf, the Word so greatly weakened the Papacy that never a prince or Emperor did such damage to it. I did nothing. The Word did it all.'

MARTIN LUTHER

CHAPTER TWO

A Crisis of the Word

'THE Word did it all . . . I left it to the Word,' said Martin Luther in that wonderful but unconvincing alibi to the effect that, when the Reformation happened, he was quietly drinking beer 'with my Philip and my Amsdorf'. The Reformation was, indeed, more than a storm in a beer mug. It shook the world and overturned kingdoms. But perhaps those reformers who lived most nobly and thought most deeply, and committed themselves to the point of suffering and death, would have agreed with Luther. Fundamentally, it was about the Word of God. To say so is not to romanticize or oversimplify, or forget the ugly elements of venality and pride, or the earthy matters of political and social existence. Nor is it to flee history for some abstract matter of theology. It is rather to see in history itself, by faith, the finger of Almighty God.

In the first place, the Word of God is—*Vox Domini*—the Voice of the Lord as Psalm 29 expresses it, shattering, explosive, majestic, the words which are deeds of the Living God. It is the Voice, as the Fourth Gospel says, of the Good Shepherd. Eivind Berggrav, that fine Archbishop of Norway, tells how when he was a boy he would go out to meet his father, who was a shepherd, on the Norwegian hills. And far off, he would hear his father's voice calling, long before he could distinguish any separate words, and this was the first, all-important thing, that he could recognize his father's voice. The theology of the Reformation, like that of the Bible, is a 'God is alive!' theology, concerned in the first place not with ideas or emotions or patterns of behaviour, but with personal encounter. Luther's own personal breakthrough came as he searched his own heart and wrestled with the Scriptures, and above all with one word 'Justice—the righteousness of God'. This he had thought to be an abstract attribute of Deity, standing over and against men in condemnation. Illumination came when he saw that it is rather the gift of God by which men live. And he goes on to say that with this clue, he turned to other attributes of God in Scripture as 'the Work of God (that which he works in us), the Power of God (with which he makes us strong), Wisdom of God (with which he makes us wise) . . .'. In other words, God is not apart from his world, as Luther said later, rather like a sleepy nursemaid rocking the cradle with her toe. Here is God Himself moving, coming creatively into human life, giving Himself in a persistent, creative energy which never ends. Dr Torrance has suggested that, for Calvin too, the primary significance of the Word is this personal encounter with the Living God.

From this encounter with the Word, comes a new proportion of faith. The great Erasmus, who kept his ear to the ground, says that in the year 1524 there were five evangelical slogans going the rounds, the words 'Gospel, Word of God, Faith, Christ, Spirit'. It is a witness how soon the new understanding of the gospel had gone from the study to the market-place. The words form a coherent constellation, a kind of Southern Cross against the background of a new hemisphere of Christian experience. Not new, in the sense that nobody had ever known them before, or that the reformers were the first who properly understood the Christian message, but new, fresh for them as in each generation it has to be found and proved anew.

First, 'Gospel'—good news about the Grace, the forgiving Mercy of God. Protestants have so beaten the doctrines of the reformers into clichés that they have sometimes obscured the vital point that the first reformers were excited about their discoveries, 'like some watcher of the skies, when a new planet swims into his ken'.

It is a return from legalism—that side of late medieval religion which Erasmus and Colet and More had trounced so savagely—what Gilbert Burnet once called 'superannuated Judaism'—to the kerugma, the marrow and kernel of Scripture, to that which, as Luther said, 'treats of Christ'. When the Cambridge Reformer, Thomas Bilney, was converted, it seems that it was one word which did it. In 1 Timothy 1[15] there is the affirmation that 'Christ Jesus came into the world to save sinners'. In the Latin Vulgate this is described as a faithful (*fidelis*) saying, but now in the new Erasmus version stood the word '*Certus*' (sure, certain)—and to him this made all the difference.

Here is the optic nerve of the Christian message, the source of its joy and wonder: God receives us because His love depends, not on what we are, but on what He is, because His nature and His name is Love.

Luther put it in a famous image. Human love, he says, is always a broken arc: it stops short somewhere, as we find we cannot love those who are ugly or evil or who do not love us. But God's Love is a perfect circle, for He loves the evil and the good: He not only loves the unworthy, but His love is able to create worth where it was not present before. This is something we can never earn, and a debt we can never repay, but to be aware of it is to begin a new life of free, spontaneous, grateful service. This is the end of legalism, of quantitative religion, of a lop-sided over-emphasis on reward and merit. The watchword 'By Faith alone' was able to act as a kind of theological Geiger-counter, a touchstone against error.

'Gospel'—'Word of God.' In this context, not so much

what we called the Voice of the Lord, as the witness to it in Holy Scripture.

Luther spoke of a twofold certainty of the Word. There is, first, the revelation in history, beginning in Israel, but culminating in the Acts of Christ for us, to which Scripture bears witness. These things happened, and nothing can ever un-happen them, and because they happened nothing can ever be the same again, and all history moves within their context. This is something plain and objective. It is like the fountain playing in the market-place—still true, still happening, even if up some side-alley the view of it is blocked by a cart or a projecting gable. Like Mount Everest—it is there. But there is also the internal certainty of the Word of God, by which God's Spirit brings this home to each individual, in the moral perception of his own conscience, the awareness that these things which were enacted publicly on the level of history are true 'for me', that they have meaning for each human life as it unfolds, and as something on which the soul may feed and grow, day by day.

Not only individual Christians, but the Church itself lives and moves by the Word of God. I remember at school the illustration of an old fairy-tale, 'How the sea became salt'—with a magic salt machine on the bottom of the ocean endlessly churning out salt until all the waters of all the oceans were impregnated. So it is with the life of the Church; worship, belief, behaviour, all pass through the Word of God, until all is touched with its savour.

The Word creates faith. When all the reformers,[1] in

[1] My use of 'reformers' is I think justifiable, but I do not mean to imply that there was a complete unanimity among them, nor would I confine the term to the eminent divines among them. I would not minimize the importance of many thousands of ordinary people, still less the deep continuities between the 16th century and the medieval Church.

one of their rare points of unanimity, repudiated an intellectual notion of faith it was because for them faith is more than an idea, more than a sentiment of confidence, that it was for them, in modern jargon, existential. That is why, for Luther, temptation, for which he used a special word '*Anfechtung*', was so important. Our life on earth is a battle school for faith, with live ammunition. Hence his famous saying, 'Not reading books or speculating, but living, dying and being damned' make a theologian.

Faith for the reformers is not, as it has sometimes been for some Protestants, a fugitive and cloistered virtue, an escape from anguish, doubt and challenge. I remember some years ago watching a long line of blue-grey warships steam out of the harbour at Malta, and being told, 'There's a storm brewing, and when there's a storm the fleet put out into it.' It is an image of what faith meant to Martin Luther on the road to the Diet of Worms, with that quality of boldness, which the New Testament calls '*parrēsia*', which caught and held the imagination of Europe. Faith is never afraid to do the new thing, for which there is no apparent precedent. 'For what I ask,' said Luther, 'is not new that faith does? Was it not a new thing when the apostolic ministry was founded? Was it not new when Abraham offered his son? Will it not be a new thing when I pass from death to life? But in all these things, it is not the novelty but the Word of God which counts.'

Faith begins at the point of conscience. Modern man, it is commonly said, has no contact with the Christian message, for he is not conscious of any deep need, still less of guilt before God. If we mean by this that men growing up in a culture still shot through and through with Christian reminiscences, have shed the inhibitions, tabus and compulsions which remain after the Christian faith has disappeared, and that, in the main, modern men are no longer vulnerable to what used to be called 'The preaching of the Law', as proclaimed, say, by Billy Graham, this might not be a bad thing. Psychologists and theologians have a work to do together at this point, if they can stop suspecting and patronizing one another. But in a profound sense this unawareness of guilt is not modern, but the plight of all men. We might go further and say that the guiltier they are the less biting is their conscience: and Eichmann and the sadistic lady gaoler at Belsen would support the view. 'The Scripture sets before us', said Luther, 'a man who is not only bound, wretched, captive, sick and dead . . . but who adds to his miseries that of blindness, so that he believes himself to be free, happy, possessed of liberty and ability, whole and alive.'

The confused, intermittent unease of men with themselves and their society may be far from being what Bunyan called 'a bruised conscience', but there was a law court in each human soul long before it appeared in the writing of St Paul. The one dogma which the historian must accept, said Herbert Butterfield, is original sin. Nobody seeing Cocyannis's terrific film of the 'Elektra' can suppose that original guilt is simply the morbid invention of the Latin Fathers, or that classical Greek tragedy (as well as Shakespeare) is concerned with ephemeral or superficial problems. We have to listen to Augustine and to Dostoievski when, with sensitivity and imagination beyond our own, they tell us of what goes on in the 'abyss of human conscience'.

What the psycho-analyst treats and what he is able to cure is important and not to be minimized but, despite his crowded appointment books and thronged waiting-rooms, he is no more able than ancient altars, and much less able than many confessionals, to persuade men that their guilt is done away.

But modern man is more sensible than many generations to corporate shame and collective guilt. The German mayor and his wife who committed suicide on the night after the Allied commander had made them walk through the liberated concentration camp at their door, which they had never seen, did not need to be Christians to feel a shame the burden of which was insupportable. The guilt of those who builded Belsen, or of the Allies who bombed Dresden and Hiroshima, the crime of genocide, the entail of generations of race discrimination, these live in the memory and actions of modern men, though perhaps more sharply imagined by poets and novelists than by the theologians. Yet the Church might begin with such statements as the Stuttgart Declaration of 1945, when the leaders of the German Church confessed their 'solidarity of guilt', and address itself to this corporate situation, without letting human responsibility be dissolved into the 'modern dilemma' or the 'human predicament'.

Sin and guilt are not primarily psychological, but they are theological words. The Bible shows us human life in a world made and ruled by the Living God. And in the murder of an innocent, Jesus of Nazareth, there is the deepest indictment of man in history, not as an isolated event, but confirming and making sense of all the cruelty, violence and wrong which disfigure human life, and which burst through and threaten all our joys and respectabilities. But this is not just a theological notion, to be received by the mind. If there is indeed a good God, we are at odds with Him as well as with one another, and if we are human beings and not simply elaborate psychological machines, then there is something which only the Maker of the universe can say to us, in the moral perception, in our self-awareness, at the point of conscience. Not long ago there was a cartoon in *Punch* which showed a monk nailing a poster to a board, and the notice said,

'Trespassers will be—forgiven!' It is in the paradox of undeserved and unexpected forgiveness that the joy of the Christian religion lies. It is why Christians sing.

Faith cannot be dissociated from the object of Faith, Jesus Christ. 'Lo, thou must form Christ within thyself, and see how in Him God sets before Thee and offers Thee His mercy . . . faith therefore does not begin with works, neither do they create it, but it must spring up and flow from the blood, wounds and death of Christ.' On another occasion Luther told the young divine, John Brenz, that faith is not just one virtue among others, or a quality of the soul. 'But in their place I put Christ Himself and I say—this is my righteousness and so I have all things in Him.' The real theological manifesto of the Reformation is the set of Heidelberg Theses which Luther debated in 1518 with their explicit 'Theology of the Cross', their affirmation that it is in Jesus Christ that men can apprehend God, and penetrate by faith through the humanity revealed in the manger and on the Cross to the knowledge of the eternal God, '*Deus crucifixus*'.

'Spirit' has the closest association with the 'Word', for it is God's own personal energy which creates and sustains the life of faith. Here Luther's is the great perception of the free, unconstrained, spontaneous character of the Christian life, the liberty of a Christian man. 'Where the Spirit is,' wrote his disciple William Tyndale, 'there it is always summer, and there are always good fruits.' It is the Spirit whose Love, shed abroad in our hearts, makes us as Luther said 'to be Christs to one another'. Later Protestants were to draw many maps of the country of the soul. But Luther gives us the compass of faith. Or rather, his is not so much a map as an ocean chart—or like those curious maps of the Western Desert in World War II where there were few markings, but simply indications that 'here the going is good . . . or bad . . . or fair. . . .'

For in the life of faith there is genuine pioneering, adventure. Nobody has ever lived where we live, at this point in time.

There is a new morality to match the new perception of faith. Love of God and man, and not written codes, are the touchstone of Christian behaviour. This is not to deny the importance of laws, of the inherited patterns and moral traditions of the past, or of society at large. But apart from the Spirit, even the Bible becomes a dead letter, and the Christian life withers into moralism or emotional pietism. Poetry has been called 'emotion recollected in tranquillity', and an important part of the life of the Church, its forms of belief, of worship, of behaviour, are of this nature. But all these things cannot substitute for renewal 'in the Spirit'. And when the Spirit is quenched, by disobedience or sloth, then the life of the Church acquires an extra skin, isolating and insulating it from the world in which lies its mission. Then the experiences of men and women in the heights of joy and depth of sorrow of ordinary existence may be nearer to the gospel than a second- or third-hand Christianity which has withered and ceased to grow. The Church and the Christian live 'in the Spirit' or not at all.

These five slogans, then, frame the new evangelical pattern and from this new understanding of the gospel came a new understanding of the nature of the Church. In the great debate in the Swiss city of Bern in 1528, one of the turning-points in the Reformation, the Protestants put forward a noble thesis:

'The Holy Christian Church, whose only Head is Jesus Christ, is born from the Word of God and in it ever abides and it hears not the voice of strangers.'

There is a similar echo of John X and the Good Shepherd passage in the lovely definition of the Church which Luther wrote in 1537:

'Thank God, a child of seven knows what the Church is, the holy believers, and the lambs who hear their Shepherd's voice.'

The Catholic historian, Joseph Lortz, has said that the 16th-century Church was externalized, legalized, secularized, to an extent which would have horrified and appalled the Church of the Apostles. That is why Luther returned to the thought of the Church as fundamentally—people—as the communion of saints. And hence to the terrible equalitarianism, the wholeness of the one People of God. '*Coram Deo*'—in that fundamental situation where we encounter God and are received by His mercy—'there is neither priest nor layman, canon nor vicar, rich nor poor, Benedictine, Carthusian, Friar Minor nor Augustinian, for it is not a question of this or that status, degree, order'. Compared with this, all other distinctions in the Church are outward things, what Luther calls 'masks' or '*larvae*' (we might recall the masks which the actors in classical Greek drama wore). So when Luther's old colleague and friend, Nicholas Amsdorf, was called to be the Prince Bishop of Naumburg, he was troubled about wearing a mitre. Having swallowed the camel of the historic episcopate, he now strained at an hat.

But Luther told him not to worry. He might, in Christian liberty, wear three mitres, one on top of the other. Hence the priesthood of believers, the concern of all Christian men for the welfare and reform of the Church. John Knox wrote:

'I would ye should esteem the reformation and care of religion no less to appertain to you because ye are no kings, rulers, judges, nobles, nor in authority. Beloved brethren, ye are God's creatures . . . and this is the point wherein I say all men are equal.'

It was, therefore, theologically fitting for the layman to take in hand that reform of the Church which the clergy had failed to initiate. And how many and various they were and from all layers of society: from the statesmen and the civic officers, Vadianus, Spengler, Thomas Cromwell, to physicians and lawyers, artists, gentlemen and servants, from noblemen like Caspar Schwenckfeld and Von Hutten and Philip of Hesse, from the jobbing gardener, Clement Ziegler of Strasbourg to the cobbler, Hans Sachs of Nuremberg, or the poet, Nicholas Manuel of Bern, and the artists like Albrecht Dürer and Matthias Grünewald. There is Vadianus, the emblem of the 'godly magistrate' and leading laymen. And John Kessler, his friend, the image of the worker-priest, plying his trade as a saddler, but in the evening, leading those Bible classes which were the heart of the reform in his little Swiss city, until at last called away to be schoolmaster, preacher and eventually bishop. And there are the women—among them prophetesses and preachers, like that wife of the architect of Zwickau of whom the authorities wrote in despair, 'This woman simply cannot remain silent!' And then the parsons' wives: Katherine Luther with her wit and commonsense: Mrs Matthew Zell of Strasbourg, organizing soup and blankets for refugees: the second Mrs Bucer, who married four reformers in turn, and whose offspring represent a history of the Reformation in several small volumes.

But this recovery of the theological dignity and importance of the laity, and of its ministries, was compatible with a new stress of the importance of the ordained ministry, of an essential ministry of shepherding and cure of souls, the Christian pastor with, on his right hand, the Preaching of the Word, and, on his left, the administration of the Sacraments, and in his heart the pastoral office. Read Professor Tappert's fine anthology of Luther's 'Letters of Spiritual Counsel' and see how much the cure of souls mattered to him, how through the years he drew from the long travail of bearing the sins and sorrows of his people a store of wisdom and comfort. And for all

Calvin's stress on the lay elder, how moving is his concern for the dignity and majesty of the pastoral office: that brotherhood of ministry of which the noble 'compagnie des pasteurs de Genève' became the living emblem.

Against the too introverted piety of monasticism and an exaggerated other-worldliness, Luther returned to and practised a holy worldliness, in his emphasis on the fact that for most Christians, for most of the time, the way to heaven must be in the world and in our home and our job and the society around us:

'Thou that ministerest in the kitchen and art but a kitchen page,' said William Tyndale, 'know that God put thee in that office . . . if thou compare deed and deed, there is indeed a difference between washing dishes and preaching of the Word of God; but as touching to please God, none at all.'

Then there is a theology of the natural order, which is not the same as natural theology. Behind this there is perhaps a debt to the long German mystical tradition with its profound and often beautiful awareness of the God who is at the 'ground of our being' so that, as Luther said, the whole of God is wholly present in the smallest leaf or in a nutshell. And there is that astonishing 'Gospel of All Creatures' which passed from Thomas Müntzer to the first Anabaptists, the thought that the world of nature, as well as the Bible, is a book through which God teaches men, as Jesus taught through His parables the good news of the Kingdom.

Or there is the new awareness of the universe in such humanist reformers as Sebastian Münster who, in middle age, gave up the study and teaching of Hebrew for what he called 'the more serious study of geography'. And that other historian and geographer Vadianus and the fine tale of how he took his pupils and friends up a mountain to view Halley's comet, pointing out to them the stars and planets and the machinery of the heavenly bodies, until at last the cry burst from his lips, 'Ah, how I long to see the wonderful Creator of all this'.

And what we might call the D. H. Lawrence side of Luther (as well as of the great Anglican Homily 'Against Whoredom and Uncleanness') which too many mealy-mouthed Protestants have passed over with blushes, but like the following startling extract from Luther's 'Table Talk':

'We are just in the dawn of the life that is coming, for we are just beginning to recapture the knowledge of the creatures which we lost through Adam's Fall. We have a deeper insight into the created world than we had under the Papacy. Erasmus isn't curious at all about how the fruit grows in a mother's womb, he knows nothing about the worth of marriage. But we are beginning, by the grace of God, to understand God's great works, and His goodness in a single flower. So we praise Him and thank Him; in His creation we acknowledge the power of His Word: "He spake and it happened." So in a peach stone—the shell, even though it is very hard, must at its given time, open to reveal the soft kernel.'

Sermons in peach stones indeed. There, the Word of God! Thus the Word joins nature and grace, creation and redemption, in one saving creating action. No wonder that for most of the Reformers a key text was the word of Isaiah 55:

'For as the rain cometh down, and the snow from heaven, and returneth not thither, but watereth the earth and maketh it bring forth and bud, that it may give seed to the sower and bread to the eater: so shall my word be that goeth out of my mouth: it shall not return unto me void, but it shall accomplish that which I please; and it shall prosper in the thing whereto I sent it.'

CHAPTER THREE

A Crisis of Communication

THE Reformation was a crisis about the Word of God; it was also a crisis of communication. For the living Word of God addresses men at each changing moment of their life, in each changing culture and succeeding age. One way and another almost all the great works of the reformers were concerned with this, to let the Word go free, to come intelligibly home to the minds of men. It was, therefore, concerned with hermeneutics, with the Bible and with its exposition, in exegesis and in preaching and teaching.

First, the Bible itself: sometimes, as in the case of Luther's Bible, Tyndale's New Testament and the Czech Bible and the Authorized Version, a monument of beauty striking deep into the language and life of nations. But above all speaking directly to men, through the power of the Holy Spirit, self-authenticating, a kind of 'Do it yourself' Christianity, working at all levels of society from the lovely vellum New Testament, which Queen Anne Boleyn loaned to the ladies of the court, to the copy which the boy Mekins hid under the stable straw until he could read it dangerously by candlelight, and in secret.

And not only the new Bibles printed in many hundreds of thousands, but with them illustrations—some of them not much above the quality of a strip cartoon, some of them splendid and beautiful—but a reminder to our own age, that it is no good having a 'Feed the Minds' campaign unless you have a 'Feed the Imaginations' campaign alongside. And then the helps to Bible study—the

Paraphrases of Erasmus, copies of which were chained in English churches, or the simple expositions by Martin Luther and Ulrich Zwingli, which did for that age what J. B. Phillips and William Barclay have done for ours, giving old stories little new, dramatic surprises, moralizing a little here and there, kindling the imagination of faith for sluggard minds. Behind the new Bibles there was the scholarship of the biblical humanists, the tools of the revived sacred languages, of Greek, Hebrew, and a renovated Latin: the exegetical reference to the exact grammatical context and the appeal to the best manuscripts, the search for the best and truest text. And a return to the simpler, more biblical, theology of the early Fathers of the Church against the too intricate systems of the later schoolmen.

Thus the Bible was allowed to speak for itself, and men listened to it freshly, thinking themselves into the ways of thought of the Bible world. In the 1520s in Wittenberg, in Basle, in Zürich and in Strasbourg, the situation was not unlike that depicted by John Milton in Puritan London:

'Behold now . . . this vast city, a city of refuge, the mansion house of liberty . . . the shop of war hath not there more anvils and hammers working, to fashion out the plates and instruments of armed justice in defence of truth, than there be pens and heads there sitting by their studious lamps, musing, searching, revolving new notions and ideas wherewith to present, as with their homage and their fealty, the approaching reformation.'

In their studies and their lecture-rooms, Luther, Melanchthon, Zwingli, Oecolampadius, Capito, Lambert, Bucer, worked at a pace and with a rhythm which was reckless to the point of being slap-happy, but which reflected the new urgency of the age of printing. Nor were these things intended only for the learned. We know that Oecolampadius lectured in Basle to an audience of over

400 citizens as well as in his Latin lectures to the scholars. Nor may we forget the lasting influence such teaching had on the students who went out to all parts of Europe, as harbingers of Reformation, or who, like John Kessler, passed on to the common people the lessons he had learned in the lecture-room at Wittenberg. And if the commentaries were sometimes edifying rather than learned, with little survival value, to be taken up into the much more impressive biblical commentaries of John Calvin in twenty years' time, in the 1520s they were of signal value and deep importance.

And with a new kind of exegesis and comment, a new kind of preaching. Sometimes, as with Luther and Calvin, breaking the Word into daily bread for the souls of common men, livened as in Luther's case with humour and simple beauty, or as in the case of Hugh Latimer's striking home into the conscience, or inspiring and rousing like those sermons of John Knox of which an English ambassador wrote that they 'put more fire into men's bones than the noise of 500 trumpets or a thousand drums'. Or Zwingli, preaching month after month, year after year, to an audience that included almost all those who made the life of his great city tick, and adjusting the Word of God to the public and private life of a Christian commonwealth. So that when on the frontispiece of his tracts he inscribed the evangelical invitation 'Come unto me . . .', it was a proper symbolism of the fact that the whole life of a great community should be a sounding board for the promise of the Gospel.

The Catholic historian, Philip Hughes, has striking words of the effect of the Bible upon common people in that age, for he writes of the tradesmen martyrs who made the majority of the victims of the Marian persecutions:

'Through their habitual frequentation of the Bible, these people have themselves become transformed into scriptural figures, and al the drama of their lives has itself become transformed into a scriptural event, itself a continuation of the sacred story.'

He intends this as an ironical comment, but it is perhaps an unconscious testimony to a deep truth that, through the Word of God, believers do in fact become part of the divine '*Heilsgeschichte*', bearers of the Word and participators in the continuing drama of salvation.

Beside the Bible, and biblical helps, there were the tracts and edifying discourses, some of them, like Luther's, circulating in great numbers, pirated by other printers and reprinted again and again. At one time Luther kept three presses on the go, and they snatched the paper from under the pen while the ink was not yet dry. Much of this was polemical, and much of it ephemeral and much of it second-rate, but there was light as well as heat and sound, and now and then a tract of enduring beauty which has lasted through the centuries.

Like ours, that was an age of educational revolution. Here humanism and reformation overlapped. It is no disparagement of the best medieval teaching and devotion to assert that here was a new and better pattern. Dr Joan Simon says:

'Beneath the pressures of current politics and fears of social disorder, which stimulated so much state intervention in education, there always ran a clearer stream—the deeply held belief that all God's children have the right to read and understand God's Word . . . at the close of the 16th century teaching was attaining a new status and there were dedicated teachers who took a pride in their profession.'[1]

Christian education in that age was a threefold alliance of home, school and church. One of the first applications of the doctrine of the priesthood of all believers was to this duty of Christian parents to bring up their offspring in the nurture and admonition of the Lord.

'Ye be in your own houses,' said John Knox, 'Bishops

[1] *Education and Society in Tudor England*, 1966, 403.

and Kings . . . let there be worship of God, morning and evening.' The official liturgical publications of Elizabethan England made provision for such family prayer, morning and evening. The 'Order for the Day' of Martin Bucer's household in Cambridge laid down that the two theological student boarders were to catechize the maids, and we may guess it was the most pleasant of their household duties.

When it came to instruction of this kind, the reformers did not start from scratch. There were many handbooks of instruction for the devout and literate, in England the 'Primers'' simple expositions of the Creed, Lord's Prayer and Commandments, while on the Continent the so-called 'Hortuli Animarum' provided handy compilations of prayers and scripture. The reformers had not to create but to adapt an existing literary form.

None the less, the reformers had to cope with ignorance and incompetence on the part of the clergy. The horror of Bishop Hooper at the ignorance of the clergy of his diocese in the reign of Edward VI echoes what Luther had written twenty years before—'What misery have I seen . . . how the common man knows nothing at all about Christian doctrine, especially in the villages—and unhappily many pastors are quite unskilled and incompetent to teach.'

In our time catechisms are at a discount, as well as learning by rote, but it is important to observe how much they counted, in the 16th century, as a method of communication. Catechetical teaching had, as the reformers knew, a respectable pedigree:

'This is the plainest way of teaching, which not only in Philosophy Socrates, but also in our religion Apollinarius hath used; that both, by certain questions, as it were by pointing, the ignorant might be instructed; and the skilful put in remembrance, that they forget not what they have learned.'

And at least the first Reformation catechisms were called by a modern enough word 'Dialogue'. They are, of course, frozen food, which is no substitute for fresh, even when warmed up. But if it is still permissible to suppose that there is a core of mathematics and of language, which at some time must be remembered and learned by heart, then there is something to be said for learning a staple of theology and ethics when young, and disposing of this at a time when all learning is a bind!

Perhaps the earliest Reformation catechism is that of Wolfgang Capito of Strasbourg (turned into English by William Roy) and entitled a 'Dialogue between a Father and his Stubborn Son'.

It led to a curious, short-lived tradition in which it is the child who puts the questions and which came to a climax in the long-winded document compiled by Thomas Becon, in which the son begins by saying, 'I humbly desire you, Father, to consider my young age', to which the Father replies:

> 'Thy age is young: thy years are few:
> thy continuance in study is small:
> for as yet thou art not six years old.'

Then he goes on for 400 folio pages to tell his son all that a young Christian needs to know. The English Reformer, George Joye, tells how he taught a boy named Dick Purser:

> 'And as for Dick Purser, verily the child lay with me that little while and fetched me meat, whom I taught to say by heart his Pater Noster, Ave, and Credo in English with two prayers following in the Ortulus Animae—to say them in the morning and evening and this in good faith.'

The boy King, Edward VI, wrote a tract dedicated to the children of England dilating on the joys of biblical literacy and beginning, 'Ye tender babes of England . . .'. We do not know if, in the West of England, his words caught the ear of an infant Francis Drake or Richard Grenville, crying 'Ha! Ha!' among the porringers. But we do know how in later life they kneeled devoutly at Communion on the eve of the Armada, and that Drake read from the Bible and *Foxe's Book of Martyrs* as his ship nosed into the Pacific, and this may be one reason why Elizabeth's bishops were a poor lot in comparison with her sea captains.

Luther's children's catechism is a classic, a marvel of lucid simplicity, and from it he and his wife were content to make their own prayers to the end of their days, as in later years millions of others have done. Or there is that noble theological document of the Reformed Church, the Heidelberg Catechism, setting, as Karl Barth has pointed out, the whole of the Christian obedience under the key word 'Gratitude'.

Teaching in the home by the Christian parent and in the Church by the parson, was continued in the school. It was an age of new schools: in Germany, stemming from the teaching of Luther, with the planning and the programme by Melanchthon: in Strasbourg, the fine school of Jean Sturm, supported by Martin Bucer: and in Geneva, the work of Calvin and of Beza. In England many new foundations stemming in part from the new philanthropy, and assisted by the initiatives of the Tudor state. An age, too, of notable headmasters: Myconius, Platter, Ascham and Colet, with new programmes blending the ideas of Erasmian humanism and the Reformation.

It was recognized that Christian education involves much more than imparting Christian ideas or religious information. John Bradford once reminded a congregation how, at school (in Catholic days), they had been taught the sign of the Cross before they began their A B C, and for him, as for some of his hearers, this was something more than a religious gimmick.

The aim of St Paul's school, as defined by John Colet, is near enough to the Newsom Report to be derided as sob-stuff by some recent writers, but it drives home the cardinal point that religious education involves not only instruction, but a pattern of manners and behaviour:

'To increase knowledge, and worshipping of God and our Lord Jesus Christ, and good Christian life and manners to the children.'

At a time when schoolmasters are loudly disclaiming their responsibility for training in morals (parents having abdicated theirs a generation ago, and the Church doing too little and too late), we may profitably ponder how in the 16th century teenagers were made to heed the sublime moral platitudes of the Prayer Book Catechism, very plainly indeed, in words of one or at the most two syllables.

'What is thy duty towards thy neighbour?
To hurt nobody by word or deed. To be true and just in all my dealing: to bear no malice or hatred in my heart: to keep my hands from picking and stealing and my tongue from evil speaking, lying and slandering: to keep my body in temperance, soberness and chastity; not to covet or desire other men's goods: but to learn and labour truly to get my own living.'

No doubt much of this educational programme and its method is archaic and vulnerable. It was in a rather special sense a 'beat generation' and only an occasional voice like that of Thomas Becon, to his credit, was insistent on sparing the rod. Teaching by rote and by catechism comes under formidable criticism in the light of modern educational psychology and theories of education. But I dare say that, as so often in the history of education, the results were better than we might have expected, and that the young grew up to understand far more than on a modern view they ought to have done, and to understand very well what, on a recent psychological view, they were incapable of understanding.

The Crisis of Communication involved also the renewal

of devotion and worship, of spirituality. For the primary crisis of the Word involves not just a traffic in ideas, but the meeting between God and His people, and their active participation in the divine life of God Himself, Father, Son and Holy Spirit.

Here again, the Word of God was the touchstone of Reform, of liturgical worship which had run to seed and become over-elaborate, cluttered up with much which was trivial and unworthy. There was need for simplification, and Thomas Cranmer was able to cite the Cardinal Quignon to this effect. There is the fine story of how Martin Bucer went into the Cathedral at Strasbourg, crossing out of the liturgical books those ascriptions of the divine attributes—power, eternity, justice—which late medieval theology had dangerously pitched over against one another, and substituting the words 'Our Father'.

Recently the British Council of Churches called upon its members to make bold and creative liturgical experiments. So far we have not seen many, and most of them resemble the attempts to get 'brighter cricket' by widening the bat, or altering the l.b.w. rule. One hears of parsons altering the order of service each week, moving the position of the collection or the prayer—leaving a flock understandably irritated at never knowing on a Sunday what is going to happen. But in the British Museum you may see a manuscript of 'Liturgical Experiments', the mighty work which Thomas Cranmer wrought with that right hand which, one day, he thrust first into the fire. You may see there how long and hard he read, preparing his experiments over ten and it may be fifteen years, examining and comparing liturgies of the ancient Church with the new orders of Protestant Germany, and then translating and writing with a mind soaked in Scripture and the Fathers.

Three great works were his. First, the Communion

Service. Into the place of the God-Man there had come to intrude Ecclesiastical Man who perhaps has done more than Political or Economic Man to bedevil European history. But Cranmer's mighty line 'By his one oblation of Himself once offered, a full, perfect, sufficient sacrifice, satisfaction and oblation' he ruled out, as far as words may do, aberration and error and yet kept room for belief in a true presence of Christ and the realistic language of Scripture and the Fathers which make men aware of the awful nearness of the Blood of Christ. And then the Litany which has been called the loveliest service in our language. Two years ago I attended a theological conference in Communist Czechoslovakia, where for days American and Communist theologians hammered out the significance of the gospel for man in modern industrial society. When the Dean of Washington, Francis Sayre, was asked to close, he read the Litany—exactly tuned as it was to what is perennial and contemporary.

Those who in our time are making experiments will remember gratefully how Cranmer himself had to meet the reproach of the die-hards who thought that his new service was but a Christmas game, and they will read with appreciation his rather donnish but forthright reply beginning, 'O ignorant men of Devonshire.' What is worth remembering, too, is that within a wonderfully short space of time the new liturgy became something for which to suffer and to die. It was in double sense, brand new. Laurence Saunders read Morning Prayer to his people gathered outside his prison bars, and, on Jesus Green, Cambridge, John Hullier read from that three-year-old Communion service until his voice was choked in smoke. Cranmer's third achievement was to turn what had been the select, Latin offices for choirs, into English services for the congregation, the creative marvel of Matins and Evensong.

In this last feat Cranmer had been anticipated by the stormy petrel of the Reformation in Germany, the fiery leader of the Thuringian peasants, Thomas Müntzer. For Müntzer, too, wrote a vernacular service of Matins and of Vespers with hymns for his people. And then he wrote a Mass, which was fully choral, and for which he wrote the music, in a rather old-fashioned way. But his manifesto, a rationale and apologia for the experiments which drew thousands to the little Saxon town of Allstedt, is a remarkable work which anticipates some of the stresses of the modern liturgical movement. For he celebrated behind the holy table and he had the congregation join with him in repeating the words of consecration. He was perhaps more skilled in this field than Martin Luther, whose achievement was not mean. And Luther was a better musician, or at least he got the best and most up-to-date help that he could. One thing Luther believed, a consequence of his doctrine of Christian liberty, was that there should always be the possibility of change, and from this sprang the almost bewildering proliferation of liturgies of varying worth throughout Germany.

In Zürich, Basle and Strasbourg, too, there was a ferment of experiment, and the simpler rites of Zürich and Geneva and of Poullainus and A Lasco in Edwardian England reflect a more radical, more Puritan outlook than that of Luther.

It is hymn singing which in the Reformation most emphasizes the unity of the worshipping people of God. It has been said of Martin Bucer of Strasbourg that for him the Church is built round the hymn. The Reformation produced some fine new hymns: John Zwick of Constance was its Isaac Watts, but Luther wrote a score of noble hymns, and the Reformation produced notable hymn books, the loveliest being that of Strasbourg in 1541. Then came the rousing psalms of Marot and Beza, with their sombre, inspiring 'Marseillaise' touch of defiance which set men singing not only in churches, but in the streets and on the field of battle.

It might be thought that the Reformation added little to the literature of spirituality. And it is plain that it added little to, and indeed reacted rather sharply against, the classical mystic tradition. Its defence would have been that it was not concerned to make common men into second-rate mystics, but to set before them a plain man's pathway to heaven, through the Bible and catechism, and edifying discourses, through the preaching of the Word and the worship of the congregation. Certainly from Luther and Melanchthon through the leading reformers, and among the conventicles of the Anabaptists, we could cull a whole anthology of fine illustrations of their belief in, and practice of, the life of prayer. This is not the whole truth, however, and we have to ask questions whether the reformers did not react too sharply against a tradition of 'inward religion' which passed through the radical reformers, men like Carlstadt, Müntzer, Denck, into a Protestant underworld and was lost.

The 16th-century reformers met their crisis of communication with an astonishing measure of success. Bibles, catechisms, tracts, hymns, prayers, liturgies, here was a succession of creative achievements, some of them of classic beauty and enduring worth. They had underlying principles. The touchstone of the Word. The concern that the Gospel should be set forth in language heard and 'understanded' by the people. The assertion that the Word of God could not be bound by human fear or obscurantism, but must go daringly, boldly free. And they were sensitively aware that what they were doing was important. When their books were burned, they wrote more, and turned the circulation of them into a dangerous underground movement. Theirs were no slick experiments about which to gossip in committee and argue in a weekend conference. For these things, they knew, a man must be prepared to suffer and, if need be, to die. Which is perhaps why their works have lasted so long.

CHAPTER FOUR

A Crisis of Compassion

THEY say, and if it is not true it is excellently invented, that the Panama Canal is operated by means of a working model of the canal itself, housed in a building along its bank. Here the words and acts of a few men are linked with the machinery of the lock gates outside, and what these men say and do in that room control the opening and shutting of the gates, and enable men to pass from one half of the world into the other, and from the Atlantic into the Pacific Ocean. It is a parable of Christian worship. What Christian men say and do in their tiny buildings really moves heaven and earth, because it is joined with the Word, with the action of the Lamb of God who takes away the sin of the world, and, as they pray, grace washes away the dark waters of sin, and men are translated 'from the kingdom of darkness into the Kingdom of the son of His love'.

But if you were to cut the link between the model and the canal itself, then those men would be of all human beings the most miserable, for they would be saying and doing things unrelated to anything at all. It would be like those last hours of Berlin in World War II with Hitler down in his bunker frantically moving about on his chart divisions which did not exist. And this continues the parable about Christian worship. It has to be earthed in practical compassion, and without this the noblest liturgy and most sublime music become meaningless folly. The Writer to the Hebrews, after that magnificent imagery of his Epistle concerned with temples, priests and altars, shocks us into reality with the reminder that Christianity is not only about holy buildings, holy vestments, holy men—but 'Christ suffered without the gate'. A Church which forgets these things becomes insensitive to human need and shameful inequalities, or which simply accommodates its life and action to that of an established political and social order comes into judgement. As you stand in Leningrad in what was once a noble cathedral, now an anti-God museum, you wonder whether here is not a case in point?

In our time there are two hopeful movements of Christian renewal, the return to Biblical Theology and the Liturgical Movement. Yet, by themselves, their very success might mean a Church still more dangerously introverted and cut off from the modern world.

The Reformation was a crisis of compassion. Urgent social reforms are included in Luther's first public manifesto, his 'Appeal to the Christian Nobility of the German Nation'. The Ordinance for the Christian city of Wittenberg (1522) is true to his principles and included provision for the poor, for interest-free loans to needy artisans and became a precedent for reforms in scores of other German cities.

This concern for human need was a hall-mark of the Cambridge Reformers who began the real, religious Reformation in England. If they argued new doctrines on their walks up 'Heretics Hill' it was because at the top of it were the prisoners of Cambridge gaol. If we had to pin-point the beginning of that Reformation, we might put it in December 1525 when Dr Robert Barnes, Prior of the Austin Friars, visited a poor man thrown into prison for stealing a copper kettle worth 2*s.* 4*d.*, the property of the Church of St Edward. Barnes went to see the church warden and upbraided him for being so extreme to his brother for whom Christ died. And the next Sunday, preaching in St Edwards, and finding the man in the congregation, adamant and impenitent, he made a costly *ad lib.* and set in train events which fifteen years later brought Barnes to the fire. Another leader of the group, Hugh Latimer, won, by his silver eloquence, the favour of the King. But when the King sent for him into the gallery at Windsor after a glittering preachment, and men expected him to beg some preferment, he asked instead for the life of a poor woman under sentence of death in Cambridge gaol for murdering her baby.

This was no passing enthusiasm. Later in life, Latimer was eminent among the group of preachers nicknamed 'Commonwealth' men concerned for social justice in Edwardian England and withstanding the hard-faced men about the Earl of Northumberland. In those years he preached that amazing series of sermons, bold, outspoken to the point of recklessness, continued week by week and naming names so that the occasion had for the audience something of the fascination of a modern television serial. In the time of debasement of coinage, he mocked the government measure—'Wot ye what? I chanced in my last sermon to speak a merry word of the new shilling, to refresh my auditory, how I was like to put away my new shilling for an old groat. I was herein noted to speak seditiously.' 'He that took the silver bason and ewer for a bribe, thinketh that it will never come out: but he may know that I know it: and I know it not alone, there be more beside me that know it. Oh, briber and bribery! It will never be merry in England until we have the skins of such.' Such a sermon and such words went like a winged arrow into the conscience of one bystander, John Bradford, and brought him to a life of penitence and to a good confession crowned in martyrdom.

At the time of the Reformation, and with the dissolution of monastries and chantries, an old philanthropy disappeared and, if the new men had foreshortened horizons, were less concerned with their future reward or the fate of the departed, Professor Jordan in his three volumes has shown how many-sided was the 'New Philanthropy', how numerous the new endowments of schools, hospitals and orphanages. In Strasbourg, Martin Bucer was above most reformers, the man for others, and his first published tract (1523) was entitled 'that a Christian man should not live for himself, but for his neighbour'. Others defined the Church in terms of three dimensions: Word, Sacraments and the Discipline of Christ. Bucer added a fourth—the practice of charity. It is no accident that Strasbourg became the great city of refuge for the exiled and oppressed, as it was for the thousands of desperate refugees after the failure of the Peasant War. At the end of his life, himself an exile for conscience sake, Bucer drew up in his 'De Regno Christi', a blue-print for a Christian England beginning with a careful exposition of theological, biblical principles and drawing practical conclusions, dealing with the reform of universities and schools, but treating also of the state of the English cloth trade, of the gospel of hard work and of lawful recreation. The ideal of Zwingli was of a Christian commonwealth, and for him the great prophet was Isaiah the statesman. As in Zürich, so in Basle and Bern and Geneva, the Reformation involved a network of edicts by which a Christian magistracy reorganized public worship, but in addition made new laws for welfare and the oversight of public morals. Of this process, Calvin's Geneva was the crown, but Calvin's own concern for social righteousness extended far beyond his city, and is evidenced in a vast range of his writings and correspondence. Not for nothing did M. Léonard call him 'Calvin—founder of a civilization', while such studies as those of André Biéler have shown how Calvin's concern touched the whole range of social and economic affairs.

The reformers did not need to be told that there is a

Christian duty of involvement in society, and of solidarity with the wider community. They had not that atomistic view of salvation which comes into later Puritanism, perhaps about the time of William Perkins, by which salvation becomes a multitudinous series of individual tip-and-run raids, and by which each soul is as separated from his fellows as two billiard balls side by side. This is not to deny the ultimate isolation and loneliness of each separate human being—or the privacy of each human search for God. But Luther was not only a soul—he was a public as well as a private man, for he was a Father Prior as well as an Augustinian Friar, and he was a parish priest, and he was a D.D. pledged to defend the Word of God in public affairs as in private.

Inward religion ran immediately headlong into practical consequences. What Luther learned from the Bible, meditating in his cell, was of the order of education at Dotheboys Hall. 'C-l-e-a-n. Clean. W-i-n-d-e-r. Winder. When the boy knows this out of the book, he goes and does it.' Luther learned from the Bible and experience in his own heart that our offence before God is such that only the awful passion of the Son of God can forgive sin. Therefore, he protested against Indulgences—and the meditation of his heart moved accountants in the banking house of Fugger in distant Augsburg. By the same token, private Masses for the dead are unavailing—therefore they should cease—therefore Mass priests will be unemployed—therefore old endowments must be cancelled—therefore somebody must attend to these things, therefore the godly magistrate must intervene. A similar series of urgent, practical problems followed the theological attack on monastic vows.

The swift immersion of the Reformation in ecclesiastical, political and social problems brought its temptations. Any schoolboy knows how dangerous it may be to plug into the power rather than the light switch. The possession of spiritual influence, and moral persuasion itself, may turn into a higher kind of blackmail—like the threat of Luther to make Albert of Mainz into a laughing stock. Too easily, perhaps, the reformers found themselves listening first to the lawyers, then to the politicians, then to the generals. It is a far cry from the young Luther's 'The Word must do it . . .' to the sabre rattling of the Protestant princes of the Schmalkaldic League. When Vadianus of St Gall studied the casualty lists after the battle of Cappel, and saw the names of twenty-four chaplains, Zwingli among them, he frowned that this is not how the gospel of peace ought to be defended. It is an even further distance—the distance between Calvin, perhaps, and his successor, Beza—to that striking document lately republished, the 'Liste des Gentilshommes de l'armée protestante à Orléans, 1562'—counter-signed by Lord Cecil and evidently intended to impress Elizabeth I of the military and political importance of the Huguenot cause. Where Kingdom was divided against Kingdom, as in France and Scotland and Poland, the cause of Reformation was tossed between warring factions of the nobility. In these desperate ploys the Word of God was swallowed in a deadly hubbub which foreshadowed the even greater disasters of the Wars of Religion. Not that it was all loss. That ancient and noble kingdoms like Sweden and England should publicly acclaim the Protestant cause, and that it should colour the swelling patriotism of Elizabethan London or the struggling Dutch provinces, meant an infiltration of Christian influence not to be minimized.

That century was obsessed with fear of disorder and civil strife, of anarchy. There was a great gap between practice and theory. Theory could speak grandly as does the 'Homily of Obedience' of society as a pyramid of stations and obediences, and on this view has something of the ordered symmetry of an Italian garden. But how different was the empiric reality—how much more like the apocalyptic setting of volcanic Rotorua—with the boiling mud pools, the spasmodic geysers, the steam rising here in one place and next month in another.

Luther was pretty shrewd. He avoided being entangled in the attempt to seize power by the German knights, though on a short term it must have been a tempting alliance. And though he came to uphold the rule of his Christian Prince—he had sharp words when Frederick the Wise overstepped the limits of temporal power. But Luther spoke for most of his age when he stressed the value of peace and ordered government. 'Do you not think that if the birds and beasts could speak they would say—O ye men, you are not men but gods compared with us. How safely you live and keep your possessions, whereas among us nobody can be sure of such things for a single hour? Out upon you for your unthankfulness.'

Ordered government for Luther is a good gift of God to all his children and not only to his Christians. And though Luther did not solve any better than most of us the tension between private and public morality, at least he makes it plain that love is the origin of all righteousness, and that civic duties are the fulfilment of Christian compassion.

But to give the '*jus reformandi*', as it was called, to the godly magistrate did not go without heart-searching and criticism. When in 1528 Zwingli handed over spiritual discipline to the magistrates of Zürich, by giving them the power of excommunication, his friends were alarmed, and Oecolampadius in Basle and Bucer in Strasbourg, and eventually Calvin in Geneva, sought to set up safeguards against lay tyranny, in synods and lay elders appointed by the Church.

But there was criticism of a more radical kind. Troeltsch has spoken of two principles endemic in Church history, one of world acceptance and the other of world renunciation. Both seem to belong to the Christian witness: the Christian who serves God at the White House or at No. 10 Downing Street, and the Christian who walks with the pickets outside or sits down on the pavement. A group of Zwingli's young men, gifted academics, repudiated the whole ideal of a 'Christian' commonwealth where the magistrates might be merely nominally Christian and the community, morally and spiritually, a very mixed bag.

These Swiss Brethren became the founding fathers of those congeries of Radicals whom we call the Anabaptists. Among them there was a range of opinion about government and the use of force by Christians. At one end the formidable and learned Balthasar Hubmaier, D.D.—less an Anabaptist than a Reformer who repudiated infant baptism!—who stoutly maintained the duty of the magistrate to wield the sword (Romans 13). Opposed to him a crowd of fanatics who pin-pointed the Parousia and expected the world to end next Whitsun. In between, some who believed that there must be magistrates, but that true Christians could not participate in government, and others who thought that the whole idea of government was opposed to the gospel of the Sermon on the Mount. Nor was this merely negative criticism, for among them were experiments in Christian community and in Christian communism.

But could the principles found in Romans 13, which had long availed for a relatively static society, have meaning for a rapidly changing world? It was Thomas Müntzer who made these very verses about the sanctity of the Establishment into a revolutionary manifesto calling on the magistrates and princes to help bring in a new age.

He was a learned man, and he drew communist notions from Plato and the Acts of the Apostles. Important for him was the concept of '*Gemein-nutz*' (Commonwealth) as against the '*Eigen-nutz*'—the ruthless egoism of the age (which Shakespeare also castigated under the title 'Tickling Commodity'). He led the Thuringian peasants to disaster in 1525, but it is plausible, and easy to understand, for the Christians of Eastern Germany to see him as the prophet of their own revolutionary society. Christians who speak of involvement and solidarity must be prepared to listen to the increasing number of Christians on the other side of the Iron Curtain who believe that 'involvement' means being involved in social revolution, and 'solidarity', some measure of loyalty to a Communist régime.

Practical compassion for the Protestants of the Reformation, then, involved much more than do-gooding and being kind. They believed and practised what many 20th-century Christians, not least in Germany, have had to relearn the hard way, that the Christian message for personal salvation becomes futile unless its implications are followed up, and these extend into the whole of human life, and into the political, social and international affairs of all mankind.

PART II

The New Reformation

Siate Cristiani, a movervi più gravi non siate come penna ad ogni vento e non crediate ch'ogni acqua vi lavi.

Avete il vecchio e il nuovo testamento e il pastor della Chiesa che vi guida: questo vi basti a vostro salvamento

Non fate come agnel che lascia il latte della sua madre, e semplice e lascivo seco medesmo a suo piacer combatte.

DANTE; *Paradiso*, Canto V

Ye Christians, be more sedate in moving, not like a feather unto every wind: nor think that every water cleanseth you.

Ye have the Old and the New Testament and the shepherd of the Church to guide you: let this suffice you, unto your salvation.

Do ye not as the lamb who leaves his mother's milk, silly and wanton, fighting with himself for his disport.

CHAPTER FIVE

The Feet of the Young Men

IN a recent exhibition at the Royal Academy there was a picture entitled 'Distinguished Visitors at the Tate Gallery'. On the wall of the Tate there is a modern abstract painting, all dots and squiggles and oblongs, rather like a drop of water seen under a microscope—and facing it a group of artists famous and recognizable—Toulouse Lautrec, Van Gogh, Turner, Rembrandt, Rafael, Michelangelo—their gestures and expressions ranging from puzzlement to anger and despair. 'Is this', they seem to ask, 'the one far-off divine event to which all our creation moved?' Perhaps it would be easy, with a few strokes of the brush, to turn Picasso into Tillich, Van Gogh into Barth, Toulouse Lautrec into Kierkegaard, Turner into Maurice, Rembrandt into Calvin and Michelangelo into Luther—and then to call that abstract 'The New Reformation?'

It should be a warning to those of us who, when we read the 16th century, are on the side of the reformers, those obedient rebels—to ask whether in fact a New Reformation in our time may not find us on the wrong side? But certainly the present ferment throughout the Christian world of self-examination and self-criticism (paralleled in science and industry and almost every academic institution and discipline) is a most salutary thing. Indeed in its way it represents a small but genuine Christian recovery and victory.

I have hinted that we cannot jump from the 16th to the 20th century, or ignore the important elements in the

17th and 18th centuries which we might call an intervening crisis of integrity. Through its own failures of nerve and compassion, the Church lost its hold on two coherent human traditions, one in truth, in science, letters and philosophy, the other in social justice, traditions which by the end of the 18th century were in conscious opposition to the Church, one-sided, atheistic and anti-clerical.

But if the Church met the two storms, the New Learning and the Rights of Man, with nervous and wooden hostility, throughout the 19th century there was a growing number who saw that the mind of Christ demanded hospitable and welcoming reconciliation towards new truth. And so I say, the honesty of the present ferment reflects a situation by no means as unfavourable as we might suppose, and which is the measure of a genuine Christian recovery.

The last centuries remind us, too, that our situation differs fundamentally from that of the reformers in one important respect. In that age, most thinking men accepted the essentials of Christian faith and morals. Our situation is much more like that of the early Church as it moved out from Judaism into the '*pays de mission*' of the Hellenized and Orientalized Roman world.

Like the reformers, the first Christians gave the Word priority over communication, and that is a great lesson. Put communication first, and the Christian truths and insights become adjectival to the deep environmental influences of the surrounding culture. To demythologize the Bible and traditional doctrine may be difficult, but not impossible, and in any case the attempt has to be made. But the indispensable corollary, at the same time to demythologize the thought world of one's own age—this is like trying to find an onion by stripping off skin after skin. The danger is gnosticism, after the fashion of Marcion.

It may be expected that I should make some comment on what is called 'the new Theology' and 'radical Christianity', since some of this claims to be regarded as a 'New Reformation'. The Bishop of Woolwich sees a parallel between himself and Martin Luther, whose 95 Theses were also caught up in a publicity explosion. I wish him well. He has now only to be unfrocked, tried and condemned for high treason, to write four of the world's classics, to translate the Bible and compose a hymn book, and to write some 100 folio volumes which 400 years hence will concern scholars all over the world, and to become the spiritual father of some thousands of millions of Christians—to qualify as the Martin Luther of a New Reformation. One wishes that such weighty matters could be isolated from our modern publicity explosions. The kind of balloon-like inflation which television, Sunday newspapers, weekly journals and commentators give to whatever is sensational, controversial, and above all debunking to any kind of Establishment or orthodoxy, has been extended not only to the Beatles and James Bond, but to their theological and liturgical equivalent. This does not seem to me a healthy atmosphere. I prefer Rembrandt's 'Philosopher' as an image of how new truth appears. But it always sounds reactionary to criticize a new look, and I have a lively sense that to attack rebels is to sound like the Grand Inquisitor.

We must recognize, surely, that much of what claims to be an attempt at dialogue with modern man, is not directed to the common man at all. He would find Paul Tillich, *Soundings*, *Honest to God* no more and no less intelligible than the Tome of Leo or the Creed of Chalcedon, and dismiss the whole lot as holy codswallop. What is being attempted is to sustain an intelligent conversation within a narrow stratum of society, those intellectuals who are conversant with the more highbrow television and radio programmes and with the weekly reviews. We might almost call it a dialogue within the Muggeridge layer. This is not at all to be despised. It may be very important. Only there is nothing new about this, and in fact the current conversation going on between belief and unbelief within this layer is recondite and feeble compared with that between H. G. Wells and Bernard Shaw and the Huxleys and G. K. Chesterton and Hilaire Belloc and Dorothy Sayers, thirty years ago.

In fact, the real parallel between the exponents of radical theology is not with the Reformers at all, but with the humanist groups who preceded the Reformation. They too were groups of intellectuals, providing a cutting edge for criticism and change: at the worst, mutual admiration societies always on the edge of dilettantism, but at their best, genuine harbingers of intellectual advance. Their strength was negative criticism, as is shown by the fact that their enduring writings—Utopia, Praise of Folly, Letters of Obscure Men—are concerned with satire. Corrosive wit is a formidable weapon with which to meet the defects of a complacent Establishment, or a die-hard conservatism. But as Richard Ullmann once said to me of our own contemporary young satirists in England, America and Germany, 'Satire is the last refuge of those who funk taking up the Cross.' That is why Luther and Tyndale did not approve of reformation by means of 'railing rhymes', written by men who laughed at what was rather a matter almost past tears.

In the Acts of the Apostles we read that it was the young men who played a decisive role in disposing of Ananias and Sapphira whose epitaph, surely, must have been 'Dishonest to God'. And just now we are all conscious of the hurrying feet of the young men, who at this juncture are excited by the new ideas and the new experiments. Some, of course, are just unsettled, swept off their feet by things which they lack any kind of critical apparatus to evaluate. When a student in his second or third year in college comes to doubt all the motives of his call, comes to the point of resignation of a vocation for which he and his parents have made costly sacrifice, I am not prepared to believe that this is necessarily virtue. Despite all that can be written in defence of such actions, there is a sad casualty list and I would like to keep it as low as possible, and so, if my comments are not too patronizing and obtuse, they are intended as a contribution to what I believe to be very needful just now, a dialogue between the generations in the ministry, and I rejoice to belong to a Church where, despite much cant talk, there is such a brotherhood of the ministry as makes this at least possible.

As St John might have said: 'I write unto you, young men, because you know this present age, and because you are vulnerable: I write unto you, middle-aged, because you have learned another wisdom from hard knocks, because you are irritated at having to reopen questions that you solved for yourself years ago, and because, in your hearts, you too are unsettled by the thought that you may have missed the bus. I write unto you, supernumeraries, because you know how few are the ideas which really count, when you are packing them up for eternity.'

Because, although there is a brash minority which is impervious to any criticism, there are so many younger men for whom one has deep respect, admiration and hope, not just for their own sake but for the coming Church, I will adventure a few Polonius-like admonitions. And first 'Prove all things', put to each idea, new or old, the doubt of that fine song, 'It ain't necessarily so.' Or better, remember those beautiful lines from Dante's *Paradiso* (Canto V):

'Siate, Cristiani, a movervi più gravi . . .'

'Ye Christians be more steady, not like a feather in every wind, nor think that every water cleanses. You have the Old Testament and the New Testament and the Shepherd of the Church to guide you; let this suffice you to salvation . . . be not as a lamb who leaves his mother's milk, fighting with himself for his disport.'

And then, take the long view. Study the whole history of the last 200 years with its many profound classical writings, that period during which God has spoken through many prophets outside the Church, through Marx and Nietzsche and Freud, but also from within.

You will, of course, be reading Tillich and Bultmann and Bonhoeffer, and the spate of recent writings about the new theology. But read also at first hand, and in depth, at least some of the following: Frederick Denison Maurice, on the unity of grace and creation, on the light of Christ in other religions, on the unity of all truth in Him: and for the reminder that theology must be earthed in social action. And John Henry Newman, not least that you may remember the beauty of our English language (that daily sacrifice offered and mutilated on the altar of the Ecumenical Movement) and for the superb craftsmanship of his preaching, but because he is the prophet of Vatican II and is likely to be the real starting-place for the Dialogue between English Protestantism and Rome. And then, Søren Kierkegaard, for the debunking of all professionalisms, including that of the lay ministry, and all Establishments including the rebel one, and his reminder that it is the cost of a new Reformation which is its supreme challenge. And Karl Barth, not the early Barth whose excessive transcendentalism provoked in part our contemporary excessive immanentism. But the Barth whose exposition of the Word became the nerve of the Confessing Church. Give up reading thrillers, including religious thrillers, for six months and read the massive volumes of the Dogmatic (footnotes and all—best of all, the excursuses in small print—a tip confirmed by the great Jewish sociologist, Will Herbergh). They are indeed an undiscovered country whence few travellers return, but those who do plainly declare there is gold in 'them thar hills'.

And then, refuse to stagger from one lop-sidedness to another. 'Not only . . . but also' is a good slogan for these days. It is a mark of an English theological tradition which is perhaps sounder and more Christian than the 'Either-Or' of German theology or the rigidities of currently Teutonized Americans.

There have been times when the Church has had to fight not only for faith, but for the proportion of faith, and ours may be one. 'Not only'—'but also.' 'Not only' the ministries of the laity and experimental ministries, 'but also' the pastoral office. I have stuck my own neck out as far as the next man's to get young men set aside for experimental and new ministries, as an urgent priority of the Churches' mission. But I sometimes wonder whether some of them are not anxious to be involved in everything except chores, like learning N.T. Greek, or visiting the flock in hospital, or sweating away at sermons. At any rate I hope you will re-read in these days George Herbert's *Country Parson*, and Richard Baxter's *Reformed Pastor*, and remember that across the world there are still thousands of ministers who would say of the hard grind of their pastoral care, ''Tis worth living for this, to administer bliss, and salvation in Jesus's name', and believe there is in the end no substitution for this one essential ministry of the Church, the shepherding of souls, in the time of their wealth and of their tribulation, at the moments of birth and marriage and in the article of death.

'Not only' experiments in worship, including new forms of prayer and song, and the use of drama and ballet: 'but also' the rich traditions of Christian worship and spirituality, and the sacred Christian language to learn which, as an arduous skill, might be as up-to-date as learning Russian. And nearly as difficult. And more worth while.

Above all, let us hold to the proportion of faith in God. The classical Christian doctrine of God has about it the beauty of proportion of the Winged Victory of Samothrace and of Michelangelo's 'David'. It begins with the Hebraic insights, the Old Testament words grown out of centuries of prophecy and suffering: it grows through the New Testament with those Christian intuitions, born out of white hot, molten experience. In the next centuries, like a steel sword, it was hammered and tested by a succession of teachers and thinkers, using language of great flexibility and subtlety, whose achievement is on an intellectual level, comparable with modern atomic research.

We can criticize the scholastic theologians for many things, but not for refusing to think rigorously and logically. It is disconcerting to see how recent writers speak of the discredited medieval notions about God, when these very scholastic thinkers perfected the doctrine of analogy, the recognition that all our images of God break down, that in fact we cannot define His nature at all, but only say what He is not, or faintly guess His attributes by the 'way of eminence', the 'how much more . . .' of the gospels. Balancing this, is the great mystical tradition of the immanence of God in all creation and in the very ground of our being. Time would fail to mention the enrichment of these doctrines in 400 years, from the teaching of the reformers to theologians of the modern age, and in the worship and devout meditation of countless thousands of Christian men.

That these things should at any time be open to reinvestigation and criticism in the light of new knowledge is not a new idea. During the first centuries, almost every conceivable alternative to them was put forward impressively and often with subtlety and power. From the 16th century the doctrines of the Trinity, of the Person of Christ and of the relation between God and the universe and with the minds of men have been under fire from Socinians, Deists, Rationalists and Humanists, and within the Church from a series of Christian theologians and philosophers from Bishop Butler to William Temple, and the authors of *Soundings*. Whether the 'Death of God' writers are a contribution of weight to this great debate or a pretentious and muddle-headed gnosticism, time and others wiser than I will decide. But we at least may hold to the proportion of our faith: God near and God far off: God without and God within. We too have our reasons of the heart for saying with Pascal—'God, not of the philosophers and savants only. God and Father of Our Lord Jesus Christ.'

CHAPTER SIX

The Zeal of Thine House

A FEW weeks after the end of World War II, I went with Bishop George Bell to a house in the outskirts of Berlin. In the morning, we had driven past the broken red brick walls of the prison of Tegel, where Dietrich Bonhoeffer had been imprisoned, and heard first-hand testimony to the impression which his bearing had made on Nazi guards. Now, we drove to the Bonhoeffer home, to where a small group of sad, proud people clothed in black, were waiting. Mrs Bonhoeffer took from a drawer a tiny volume which Dietrich Bonhoeffer had left for his English friend, George Bell. And as the Bishop leaned forward and kissed her on the forehead, he read the title *The Imitation of Christ.*

Well, that is what counts most. It is indeed the only really plain and obvious meeting-point between the Old Reformation and the New: this man who practised commitment and involvement, as the reformers did, to the point of suffering, imprisonment and death, and who, like them, witnessed a joyful and good confession. But for those martyrs and confessors, it is likely that Protestantism would have faded long ago, been entirely swallowed by the political and social pressures of the succeeding age. This is the great word which Dietrich Bonhoeffer says to our age and to the coming generation. Its importance cannot be over-rated.

But perhaps his theology can. There is, I think, a sound reason why in the 'Te Deum', the 'noble army of martyrs' is flanked by the goodly fellowship of the prophets, and the glorious company of the apostles. The story of the confessing Church of the third century is a warning to us not to glamorize the theology of martyrs and confessors. What kind of a theologian Dietrich Bonhoeffer would have been had he lived to maturity and to a full and considered exposition of his own ideas nobody can tell. But on what we have before us, he would seem to rank a little above Hans Lilje and a little below Joachim Iwand—who has prophetic things to say about the relation of modern Christianity to revolution and to communism which we have to heed.

It is not callous to point out that, in the grand question for which he gave his life, Bonhoeffer, like Guy Fawkes, might have been wrong. That it is still arguable that on a theoretical view, and in an empirical view of ultimate consequences, it is wrong for Christians to participate in planned assassination. It is not clear, either, whether the whole notion of 'Christianity coming of age' and 'mature Christianity' is a new insight into the work of the Holy Spirit, or an ancient and rather deadly fallacy. In any case, it is worth asking whether ideas taken from the context of an introverted Pietism in Lutheran Germany between the Wars has prophetic meaning for an English Church situation where (apart from a fundamentalist minority) what has happened has been a recovery from pietism into a smooth and rounded mediocre worldliness, leaving no difference at all between the practising Christian and his neighbour.

When, thirty years ago, W. R. Maltby wrote of God 'who loves this human life of ours, not only as a moralist approving where it is good and disapproving where it is bad, but as a poet and artist loves it, because he cannot help loving a thing so strange, piteous and enthralling as the story of every human soul must be' and when his friend Miriam Grey asked, 'Is God interested in *Punch*?'

and answered, 'He helps to write it'—what is this, but the breaking of the pietistic dam between secular and sacred? And in Kierkegaard and Barth we can find at a most profound level the devaluation of 'religious man'.

'Not only'—worldly Christianity. 'But also'—churchly Christianity. Let us take to heart in penitence and meekness the criticism of the structured Church by writers in Holland and America. Let us rejoice in all the marks of created grace in all men and in all religions, and in men of no religion at all. But let us not romanticize the secular city either and take it at its own face value. If the man in the street has his honesties and insights, he has his errors also. Never had so many men so many great possessions as in our modern affluent societies, and what Jesus said about these things no Bultmann has ever been able to demythologize. If these things blind the spirit, and if the pure in heart see, then I should find a thousand within the Church on the road to perfection for every hundred outside. As I look at our world, I see much beside the joyous independence of scientists and artists rejoicing in the gifts of creation. I see a terrible and erupting violence which may yet be the death of us all, of which the assassination of President Kennedy, Truman Capote's *In Cold Blood* and the War Crimes Trials are symptoms. The New Cambridge Modern History seeking a label for our generation wisely chose the title 'The Age of Violence'. And alongside a mounting tide of cruelty and violence, there is the steady fading of gentleness and manners, of common honesties and public decencies, of civic integrities and the glamorizing of frightful evil. And, what is even worse, a great flood of what is simply tawdry and second-rate, cheap, nasty and ephemeral. Perhaps, we need 'not only' frontier dialogues and encounters, 'but also' a recovery of the older, simpler vocation, of the Church as the conscience of society, and as a teacher of behaviour. I have not simply capitulated to Billy Graham at this point. It came home to me in Sydney among the beatniks, in a satire theatre where young people guyed savagely the intolerable boredom of our time, and sang a song about marijuana, which brought their audience to that hushed silence which, when we hear a sermon (which it was), we knew to be, in our conscience, a Word from God. All in all, I can still understand the horror of St Paul at those without hope, and without God 'in the world', and the compassion of a greater than St Paul at the sheep, scattered without a shepherd.

Of course, we must streamline our church programme, find new energy and flexibility for activities outside church buildings. But let us not naïvely suppose that a Go-Go Christianity, all spontaneity and improvisation, will be necessarily effective either. The Franciscan movement of the 13th century was the most gallant attempt ever made to by-pass an over-structured institutional Christianity. But it was led by a group of saints, and it had at its heart an austere renunciation to which I find no counterpart ('A month in a Kibbutz, a week at Taizé') among Protestants in England or America. And mark its end: after a couple of centuries it had become on the one hand a sour Pharisaism, or so worldly that it was itself a by-word for venality and greed, itself in dire need of renewal.

Some of the criticism of the contemporary Church and its worship, from Christian journalists who appear to have no roots in hard work in any local church, is from standards which prove to be superficial and external, by any New Testament standards. When John Bradford, the Bonhoeffer of the English Reformation, was asked during his trial whether the Church is visible, he replied:

'Yes, howbeit none otherwise than Christ was on earth: we must put on such eyes as good men put on to know Christ when He walked on earth. Look therefore as Christ was invisibly known to be Christ when He was on earth, so is the Church known.'

And this is the meaning of the young Luther's 'Theology of the Cross'. We see the strength and wisdom of God in visible weakness and foolishness, and we share these things, and this contradiction as we share the Cross, as members of His body. This means that the test of a living Church is how far it bears the form of a Servant, which is a hidden form known only by faith. The Church on earth is always Cinderella, dirty and ugly among the ashes, and her history an affair of pumpkins, field-mice, lizards—and only faith can see beneath the rags the Bride adorned for her husband. The Church too is a hospital where bad people are made good, and sinners forgiven. If it is thronged by the elderly, while the mature and young go off in motor-cars, it is perhaps because when men reach the 'Bay of Storms' in their sixties on the voyage of life, and meet serious illness either singly or with their wives, theirs is an existential need. The test is not whether services are exciting, up-to-date, experimental or impressively alert to recent intellectual discussion. A tiny group of rather dull people in some down-town chapel, coping with raising inordinate sums of money to keep going a building with damp and peeling walls, unappetizing and off-putting—may still reveal all the hidden majesty of God, be where Grace is offered. I am all for experiments, for lovely new churches, for fine music, for exciting and moving liturgy. But I know that in the moment when a man's sins have found him out, or when he has to face the fact of cancer, all these things are almost completely irrelevant.

Then, with the Psalmist, he turns to the House of God, and to the People of God, however mean and small its congregation, as a hart desiring the water brooks and not in vain. This truth about the heavenly dimension of the

Church and of its worship, some of us learned from Bernard Manning whose lisping, stammering tongue is silent in the grave, but whose blessed memory endures. If one or two of our Christian journalists would re-read him, they might be purged from their acidity, and look not only at the world with compassion but with those sick and decaying institutions which first nurtured them in the admonition of the Lord.

It is indeed the duty of the Church to spend itself in mission, in caring for the world. But there is a profound truth too in the Shepherd of Hermas, where Hermas meets an old lady who grows younger and younger before his eyes, until she is young and beautiful, and of whom the Shepherd says, 'She is the Church of Christ, and for her sake the world was created'.

There is, of course, a judgement on the Church, and on the People of God. This is terribly evident in the Old Testament, in the Psalms and in the tragedy of Israel. In the New Testament the indictment of religious man reaches its peak in St Paul, who in the Epistle to the Romans shows us on the very summit of the human pyramid of disobedience, religious man, man who has heard and handled the promises of God.

What happens to the Church when it, too, betrays and denies and forsakes? It is a question which Roman and Orthodox theology has found difficult even to face. The reformers could not face it because they inherited a dualistic view of history: from the division between the godly and ungodly in the Bible, to the distinction between the elect and reprobate, which Augustine turned into a philosophy of history, the tension between the Two Cities, and which for the reformers was continued in the enmity between the True and False Church. But when we turn from this and consider Christ as the centre of two concentric circles, the Church and humanity, the question becomes acute. Newman is one of the few theologians who really do press it home in this way, and he suggests that the disobedience of the People of God in the end brings terrible disaster, the suspension of grace: or, put in Protestant terms, the Word of God ceases to be the lively Word of the Spirit and of power, but becomes dead, inert, an affair only of the outward letter and the law.

But the Bible never unchurches the Church or unpeoples the People of God. If it is a terrible calling to be within the Church, it is also glorious. Once we admit that God has called us not because of our virtue or wisdom or efficiency—the ability to be up-to-date and impressive or exciting or brilliant—but simply because in His mercy He has pitied us, then we have another measure for the life and death and reformation of the Church. That is why almost all the great prophetic voices of renewal—Augustine—and Luther—and Newman—and not least and perhaps most poignantly of all, Dietrich Bonhoeffer, have been those over whom might be written 'The Zeal of Thine House has eaten me up'—they have been not only incurably religious men, but professionally religious men, and, without such, I dare say there will be no renewal in our time, either. 'For God's Word', says Luther, 'cannot be without God's people, and God's people cannot be without God's Word.'

One feature of the Old Reformation we have not mentioned, and we must not gloss over, the polemic, the controversy on both sides of the great divide between the reformers and what they called 'Popery'. It is no use playing down the element of bigotry and intolerance. From Roger Williams and John Milton at one end and J. S. Mill and Abraham Lincoln at the other, the literature of liberty is post-Reformation and to a marked degree on the Christian fringe—here we really do meet the prophecy of unbelief. There were few reformers of a really eirenical and gentle spirit, though Martin Bucer was one, and John Foxe another. But when we have paid tribute to Luther's integrity, and to his insistence on bearing witness to truth at all cost and without compromise, it is no good making him more ecumenical than he was, and highlighting his friendly overtures to the Bohemians, for example, when he was so rude to almost everybody else who publicly differed from him. We have to ask whether, in fact, he and most others of his age were working with an idea of truth in relation to error which came into the Church during the 2nd and 3rd centuries, and hardened thereafter, and from which the modern Churches are only now struggling to be free.

But at least, tardily, we are mending our manners and our ways. No talk about a 'New Reformation' can ignore the growth and progress of the great ecumenical movement in the last half-century, with its accelerating momentum, if not more than a sign the size of a cloud on the horizon, none the less, a sign of forgiveness, and renewal. In some ways, the radical theology may be a providential counterpart to this great movement, for this vast concern for ending division and seeking unity, has necessarily involved an increase of Christian introversion at the time when it needs most to understand and adventure into mission in the world. There are signs indeed that it is benefiting from the intellectual scrutiny of organized, churchly Christianity within and beyond the Christian fringe. It will always need to be purged of a certain idealism and romanticism, as it works down to the level of the grass roots (and the more deadly upturned stone) level. It has its own perils and problems of bureaucracy, of failing to adjust itself to the problems of a recrudescent confessionalism—which to a degree is inevitable, and salutary, but might become very dangerous indeed, for it is at the world confessional level that the temptation to play ecclesiastical power politics becomes really sinister.

But already, across the world, new Churches have found this the greatest experiment of all, the adventure of commitment to a unity which involves the re-shaping and re-examination of the whole life of the Church, visible and invisible, material and spiritual. Commitment to unity is the genuine commitment to Christian revolution in our time, the paramount hope that, under God we shall find a new kind of Church for a new kind of world.

And now, there is a new voice added to the Ecumenical dialogue. A New Reformation may not be the best diagnosis of what is going on among the Protestants, but it is certainly in order for the Church of Rome. We have seen in Vatican II the brave sight of a great Church beating Protestant platitudes into Catholic epigrams, discovering freshly for themselves things which, with Protestants, have become law and letter rather than Word and Spirit.

Some months ago, tired with the contradiction of saints, in the correspondence about Unity in the pages of the *Church Times* and the *Methodist Recorder* I took comfort in the noble sentences of 'De Ecumenismo'. There is, after all, God's good time—'The Lord of Ages is wise and patient in the gracious plan that He has for sinners'.

And then, the affirmation that the Church stands in need of a threefold change. First, a renewal of its authentic mission and vocation. Second, continual Reformation. Third, conversion and a change of heart. One could take from Church History the emblems of this trinity. That for the renewal of the People of God in their authentic mission, one must turn to the Primitive Church. That for conversion and change of heart, one might study the Evangelical Revival. But that here, too, was the authentic meaning of the Protestant Reformation, not as something done once for all, to be crystallized and petrified in static memorial, but '*Ecclesia semper reformanda*'—the Church always being renewed by the Word and in the Spirit.

These things, it is abundantly clear, we can no longer hope to seek or find alone or asunder. One world in revolution needs one Church strong and united, speaking to its condition with the burning charity of Christ Himself. Perhaps this in the end is the one lesson which the reformers have for us. They, too, knew themselves to stand in a dire hour, in utter incompetence and insufficiency. But they knew where to turn and to whom to go. How can a Church be born again when it is old, save in the renewing mercy of Almighty God? Where can it find reformation, save in the Word of Christ who lives and rules? And what is a change of heart, but the moving of the Spirit, as He is evidently moving in our stony hearts, teaching us in these last days new penitence, new courtesies, new gestures of comradeship and hope, new awareness of our one mission to lost mankind?

This discussion has been much concerned with ideas and events and documents. But they were men who made the Reformation, some of them great men and a few of them giants. I see Luther as Michelangelo's giant figure of Jeremiah—the great introvert; and Calvin, as his Ezekiel, his arm gesturing towards the world, and Zwingli, assuredly Isaiah; and Bucer as Jonah, the missionary: and even Thomas Müntzer as a Daniel come to judgement. Today we need all the prophetic voices of the past. They, too, belong to the coming dialogue, perhaps one day to be recognized by our separated brethren to have been doctors of the Church.

But the most famous picture of that age is by the friend of Erasmus, and the disciple of Luther, Albrecht Dürer. It is that image of an age of Revolution and of Violence, the Four Horsemen of the Apocalypse, who in our world, too, ride again, Famine, Death and War. But with the reformers we, too, discern another in their midst, like unto the Son of Man, and His name is called Word of God, and He has on His vesture, and His thigh, a name written: 'King of Kings and Lord of Lords': and he goes forth, conquering and to conquer.